Young Troopers

Stories of Army Children on the Frontier

PAIGE RAMSEY-PALMER

D1621624

Southwest Parks and Monuments Association

TUCSON • ARIZONA

TO KIM, KRISTIN, AND CAROLYN

I WISH TO THANK my daughters for their patience and support while I worked on this project. I owe a special thanks to Jerry Yarbrough, Superintendent of Fort Davis National Historic Site, and Mary Williams, site historian at Fort Davis. Without their unwavering support, I might have neither undertaken nor completed this book. A sincere thanks goes to Neil Mangum, Trans-Pecos Historian for the National Park Service. I especially thank my parents, Max and Dottie Ramsey, who encouraged our family's passion for history. Thanks to my sister, Carolyn Cole, for helping in so many ways, and my brother, Max Jr. for always being there.

I appreciated the hospitality and assistance I received at all the forts I visited, especially from Kitty Deernose at Little Bighorn Battlefield National Monument, Harry Myers at Fort Union National Monument, and the staff at Fort Laramie National Historic Site. The staff librarians at the Denver Public Library and the archivists at the Colorado Historical Society and the National Archives were invaluable. Other professionals have been very generous with their photos and materials, including Towana Spivey of the Fort Sill Museum, Thomas R. Buecker of the Fort Robinson Museum, Alan C. Aimone with the U.S. Military Academy, James P. Finley with the Fort Huachuca Museum, and John Nielson, formerly of the Fort Concho Museum, as well as numerous others.

Finally, I wish to thank the descendants of these families who saved their memorabilia and letters, and the National Park Service who has made the information available for us all to use.

FIRST EDITION

Copyright © 1997 by Paige Ramsey-Palmer
All rights reserved.

Edited by Ron Foreman
Book design by Larry Lindahl Design
Archival photo research by Kathleen Bryant

Picture credits on page 64

Library of Congress Cataloging-in-Publication Data
Ramsey-Palmer, Paige.
    Young troopers : stories of army children on the frontier / Paige Ramsey-Palmer. –1st ed.
        p. cm.
    Summary: Presents accounts of experiences of soldiers and their families serving on the Western frontier during the latter half of the nineteenth century.
    ISBN 1-877856-68-1
    1. Frontier and pioneer life – West (U.S.) – Anecdotes – Juvenile literature. 2. Children of military personnel – West (U.S.) – Biography – Anecdotes – Juvenile literature. 3. West (U.S.) – History – 1848-1860 – Anecdotes – Juvenile literature. 4. West (U.S.) – History – 1860-1890 – Anecdotes – Juvenile literature. 5. United States. Army – Military life – History – 19th century – Juvenile literature. 6. Indians of North America – West (U.S.) – History – 19th century – Anecdotes – Juvenile literature.
    [1. Frontier and pioneer life – West (U.S.) 2. United States. Army – Military life. 3. West (U.S.) – History.] I. Title.
F596.R359 1996
978 – dc20   96-35089
                                                                                          CIP
                                                                                          AC

Contents

BACKGROUND:
Officers and families,
Brechemin House,
Fort Laramie,
Wyoming Territory

Charles E. Fearn lived with his parents at Fort Lowell
near Tucson, Arizona, from 1885 to 1886.

Tall in the Saddle

DAVID BIDDLE LEARNED TO RIDE a horse bareback when he was four years old. A year later he graduated to a saddle with stirrups and a bridle. Still, five-year-old David was rather young to go riding off into the wilderness with the troops. Yet that is exactly what he got to do in March 1873.

Although representatives of the army were trying to make peace with the Modoc Indians in northern California, Captain James Biddle and the Sixth Cavalry were ordered to Fort Bidwell to be ready to help in the Modoc Wars. Captain Biddle's wife, Ellen McGowan Biddle, was still recovering from a difficult childbirth during the winter and was unable to care for David. The captain decided to take his young son with him, feeling certain that the trouble would be settled by the Peace Commissioners and his column would have to travel no farther than Fort Bidwell.

Captain Biddle outfitted David with a little union suit, wool flannel shirts, heavy corduroy jacket, riding pants reinforced with

ABOVE:
The rugged lava beds by Tule Lake provided cover for both Indians and soldiers during the Modoc Wars.

buckskin, and leather boots. On a winter expedition like this, one could not dress too warmly.

When the Sixth Cavalry reached Fort Bidwell, they received orders to ride immediately to the lava beds by Tule Lake, near the California-Oregon border, where the Modocs were making a stand. Captain Biddle had no choice but to take young David along.

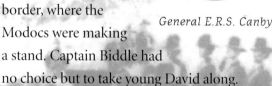

General E.R.S. Canby

Before the troops could confront the Modocs however, they had to battle the weather. On the trail to Tule Lake Captain Biddle's column was caught in a terrible blizzard. For twelve days they struggled through snow so heavy and cold that three soldiers froze to death.

At Tule Lake efforts to get the Modocs to surrender peacefully failed when the Modoc leader, Kintpuash ("Captain Jack"), murdered General E.R.S. Canby. On April 15th the army attacked the Modoc stronghold and succeeded in cutting them off from access to water in Tule Lake.

The battle became a siege that lasted for weeks. David decided to take up fishing to pass the time and provide some relief from the boring army menu of beans, jerked beef,

THE MODOCS

The Modoc Indians of northern California were considered a peaceful and helpful tribe by early white settlers. They made baskets, dwellings, and boats from the reeds of Tule Lake.

MODOC LEADER, KINTPUASH ("CAPTAIN JACK")

Hunters and trappers, the Modocs dressed in buckskins, furs, and cloth made of bark. It wasn't until the discovery of gold and the resulting mass migration of whites that tensions began between the Modocs and white settlers.

and hardtack biscuits. Tule Lake seemed like a safe enough place to fish.

David was joined by a young Indian friend, the son of one of the Warm Springs Indian scouts. Just as the boys were casting their lines from the lake shore, they heard gunfire and bullets whizzing past their heads.

Bang! Zing! Someone was shooting at them!

"Modocs!" David's companion shouted. The Indian boy dropped his fishing pole and ran.

But David had something on his hook and was not about to leave his pole or the fish behind. Ignoring the soldiers' shouts to take cover, David calmly landed his fish and grabbed his pole before dashing to safety. Fortunately for David, he could fish better than the Modoc snipers could shoot that day.

BACKGROUND: Army troops in formation during Modoc Wars

THE MODOC WARS

In 1864 leaders of the Modoc agreed to leave their homelands and live on a reservation with other tribes, some their traditional enemies. Kintpuash, a Modoc leader the whites called "Captain Jack," didn't like the reservation. After he and sixty or seventy families returned to their former homes, the cavalry was sent to negotiate with them. On a November morning in 1872, negotiations erupted into violence. The Modocs fled. For four months, Kintpuash and sixty warriors held off the army, hiding in "Captain Jack's Stronghold," a series of caves in the Tule lava beds. The conflict led to Kintpuash's assassinating General E. R. S. Canby. The army responded by capturing

"CAPTAIN JACK" SHOOTING GENERAL CANBY

Kintpuash and three other Modoc leaders, hanging them, and sending their heads to the Army Medical Museum in Washington. The rest of the Modoc warriors were sent to what is now Oklahoma, where they were forcibly dispersed among other tribes.

INDIAN SCOUTS

The army soon learned that Indian warriors had one great advantage—they knew the countryside. In order to keep up, the army employed scouts. Sometimes Indians worked with the army in battle against other Indians because they were struggling against the same tribes the army was trying to contain. Scouts might even be from the same tribe the army was fighting, if there were rivalries within the tribe.

BELOW: AN INDIAN SCOUT

David's father decided one close encounter with hostile Indians was enough for his son. For the rest of the campaign David stayed in camp.

During the four-month campaign, David's father was promoted to the rank of Major. David got a promotion of sorts, too. His Warm Springs Indian friends fashioned a handsome new buckskin outfit for him to replace the clothes he had worn out, or perhaps outgrown. Certainly David rode a little taller in the saddle on the way home. When Major Biddle's command arrived home, Mrs. Biddle could hardly recognize her not-so-little boy.

Mini-aku's Wish

FOR MINI-AKU'S PEOPLE, the Brule Sioux of the northern plains, life had changed a lot since white men from the East had come. Mini-aku didn't think all those changes were bad. Like her father, Chief Spotted Tail, she believed it would be better for her people to cooperate with the newcomers than to oppose them.

For the Brule Sioux, armed conflict was nothing new. Generations before the white men came, Mini-aku's people had fought the Pawnees and other tribes for control of hunting grounds on the prairie.

Indeed, Spotted Tail had become chief by leading Brule Sioux warriors in battle. His people respected his courage and his willingness to sacrifice his own freedom for the greater good of the tribe. While serving time in the military prison at Fort Leavenworth, Kansas, he saw the huge supply depot there and realized that the U.S. Army was far more powerful than his people could have imagined.

Spotted Tail knew that his people could fight for justice but, in the end, the might of the army would defeat them. It was useless

ABOVE:
Chief Spotted Tail

to resist such a force, he concluded. Thus, the chief urged his people to follow the path of peace.

Even with the prospect of peace in Wyoming Territory, the people of Fort Laramie and Spotted Tail's tribe still faced a common enemy: disease. In March 1866, tuberculosis claimed Mini-aku. She was only eighteen. Her last wish was to be buried at Fort Laramie.

The journey from Spotted Tail's winter camp to Fort Laramie took two weeks. A messenger rode ahead to ask Colonel Henry Maynadier, commanding officer of the fort, if Mini-aku's wish might be granted. The colonel said the post would be honored. As the grieving father and his band approached the fort, Colonel Maynadier and his senior officers rode to welcome them.

Mini-aku's body was wrapped in smoked deerskin, covered in a buffalo robe, and placed in a simple pine casket made by the soldiers. The troops also honored Brule Sioux custom by erecting a nine-foot-high wooden platform, or scaffold, on which to lay Mini-aku to rest.

Soldiers and their families joined several hundred Brule Sioux in the funeral procession. The post chaplain

THE GREAT SIOUX NATION

Rival tribes gave the Sioux their name, which in one language meant "snake," and in another, "cutthroat." The Sioux know themselves by the names of their bands, such as Hunkpapa, Yankton, Oglala, Brule, and others. They are also known by the dialects they speak, Lakota, Dakota, or Nakota. Long ago the Sioux were a farming people, but they were forced west to the plains by other tribes. In the vast territory of the plains, they became hunters who traveled according to season. They developed stunning horseback skills, racing after great herds of bison. Buffalo was their primary source of game and a major influence on their spiritual beliefs.

LEFT: A BRULE SIOUX VILLAGE IS GUARDED BY SOLDIERS.

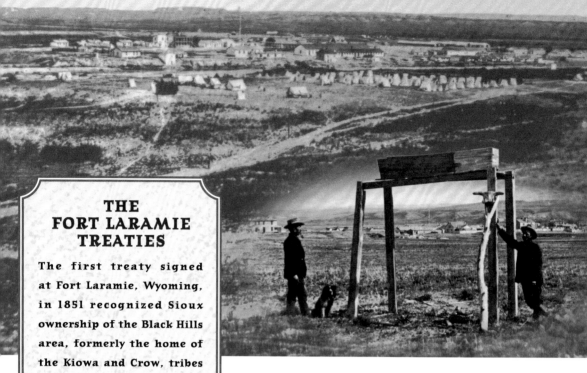

THE FORT LARAMIE TREATIES

The first treaty signed at Fort Laramie, Wyoming, in 1851 recognized Sioux ownership of the Black Hills area, formerly the home of the Kiowa and Crow, tribes the Sioux had pushed out. Whites began to travel across Sioux land as settlers moved west, and the army built forts to protect them. Red Cloud, Crazy Horse, and others fought against the incursions. On April 29, 1868, a second treaty was signed at Fort Laramie, Wyoming, yielding the Bozeman Trail and increasing the Sioux lands to the west. The treaty said: "From this day forward all war between the parties to this agreement shall forever cease. The Government of the United States desires peace, and its honor is hereby pledged to keep it."

ABOVE: Fort Laramie in 1870
INSET: The burial scaffold of Mini-aku

offered a prayer, which an interpreter translated to the Indians, and medicine men performed traditional last rites.

Mini-aku's burial platform stood for years at Fort Laramie as a fitting memorial to her father's dream of peace. Unfortunately, that dream proved to be no more than a wish. Before the summer was out, Plains Indian tribes and the U.S. Army were warring again.

Fighting would drag on for another generation. Many thousands of men, women, and children on both sides would be killed before all western tribes finally accepted the inevitable: White men and women had come to the western plains to stay.

Crazy Head

MISUNDERSTANDINGS can happen when people don't speak the same language or share the same culture. Major Andrew S. Burt knew that encounters with Indians could be peaceful as long as both sides were willing to give a little. But, as his family discovered, sometimes compromise just is not possible.

In 1867, the Burt family traveled west on the Oregon Trail from Fort Kearny, Nebraska, to Fort C.F. Smith in Montana Territory. One morning they met a party of Crow Indians.

While Major Burt and the Crow band's chief, Crazy Head, exchanged friendly greetings, the chief's wife gestured that she wanted to hold the Burts' baby daughter. Not wanting to appear impolite, Mrs. Burt reluctantly agreed and handed the infant to the Indian woman.

ABOVE:
Crow (Apsalooke)
men carrying a
coup stick

Seeing how much the fair-haired child pleased his wife, Crazy Head motioned to his herd of ponies and held up both hands twice.

Ponies. Twenty. The meaning of the chief's sign language slowly dawned on Major Burt. Crazy Head wanted to make a trade: Twenty ponies for the Burts' baby girl.

THE OREGON TRAIL

Stories of rich land tempted easterners to Oregon, and in 1841, the first wagon train headed west from the Kansas prairies. Families traveled in "prairie schooners"—covered wagons—led by teams of oxen or mules, covering fifteen to twenty miles a day. The

WAGONS AT FORT KEARNY

wagons were filled with provisions and cherished possessions. Livestock was herded by men on horseback. Hardships included frequent breakdowns, river crossings, buffalo stampedes, Indian attacks, rough country and bad weather, and diseases such as cholera or scurvy. Travelers had about five months to complete the long journey and reach the western high country before winter snows began. Army forts along the trail offered shelter and protection.

"No," Major Burt replied firmly. He quickly snatched his little girl out of the arms of Crazy Head's wife.

Crazy Head held up his hands three times.

"No!" the major shouted, handing the baby to his wife.

Mrs. Burt clutched her baby and rushed into the tent. Meanwhile, Crazy Head continued to negotiate. How many ponies did Major Burt think his baby was worth?

THE CROW

The Crow were one of the tribes of the Great Plains. They became known as daring raiders and brave warriors, and though they fought fiercely against neighboring Plains tribes, they never waged war on whites. This decision rose not out of admiration for whites, but out of their need for an ally against the Sioux. They signed treaties with the U.S. government and joined the U.S. Army as scouts in the war against the Sioux, their common foe.

ABOVE: CROW (APSALOOKE) PARTY

Finally, the chief pointed to his wife. Would Major Burt take her in trade?

"No, No, No!" the major barked.

Having failed to make a deal, Crazy Head and his band moved on.

Major Burt wondered aloud if the chief really had been willing to trade his own wife for the Burts' baby, especially since she was the one who had admired the baby in the first place. Could the chief have been joking all along? Either way, Mrs. Burt was glad to see the Crows leave.

Andy's Shock

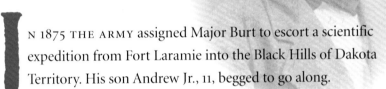

I N 1875 THE ARMY assigned Major Burt to escort a scientific expedition from Fort Laramie into the Black Hills of Dakota Territory. His son Andrew Jr., 11, begged to go along.

"Why not?" thought Major Burt. After all, the team of scientists only planned to pan for gold and make maps of the area. How dangerous could it be?

Andy loved being out in the field, far from civilization and close to nature. Away from the confines of the fort, everything seemed larger somehow.

Soldiers always seemed to know just what to do in any situation, Andy thought. He could trust them. And he looked forward to the day he could be a real soldier, too.

One day, at about dusk, the soldiers were caught in a terrible thunderstorm. In the half light and driving rain, Andy lost sight of his father. When he saw several troopers heading for the shelter of a huge tree, Andy followed them.

The boy had seen plenty of storms before but none as fierce as this. The wind was so strong it seemed to be raining sideways.

ABOVE:
Andrew Gano Burt
Jr. about age ten

THE BLACK HILLS

The Black Hills, or *Paha Sapa*, are the sacred land of the Sioux. The 1868 treaty signed at Fort Laramie granted these mountains, rich with trees and streams and game, to the Sioux. But when gold was discovered in the Black Hills in 1874, prospectors poured in, and U.S. troops were dispatched to keep the situation under control. Two years later, Sitting Bull's people and their Cheyenne allies won the Battle of Little Bighorn. But victory was short-lived. Within a few years the Black Hills were reclaimed by an act of Congress, the great buffalo herds were killed off, and the traditional ways of the Sioux were gone.

PICTURED: AN ENCAMPMENT IN THE BLACK HILLS DURING THE
U.S. ARMY EXPEDITION LED BY GENERAL GEORGE A. CUSTER IN 1874

ABOVE:
Long lines of supply
wagons followed
Custer's expedition
into the Black Hills.

Awesome lightning turned night into day. The deafening thunder spooked the horses, and the soldiers struggled to control them.

Flash! Boom! In an instant a great bolt of lightning struck the tree under which Andy and the men had sought shelter. The lightning raced down the trunk and roared through the barrel of a rifle leaning against the tree.

The rifle stock shattered, and the lightning bolt split in two. The larger part of the bolt struck and killed a horse nearby. The other bolt struck Andy on his cheek, passed through his body, and exited through the side of his shoe, "leaving a hole as large as a dime." Andy's world went black.

Major Burt came running. He found Andy unconscious but still breathing. It took more than an hour for the expedition's doctor to revive the boy.

Andy made a remarkable recovery, although the shock permanently damaged his left eye. His dreams of becoming a soldier died on that trip, but at least Andy lived to tell about it.

BELOW:
1879 Winchester
38-caliber
carbine with
octagonal barrel

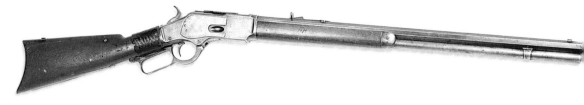

Mud Rain and a "Hopper" Circus

I N 1871 LIEUTENANT CHARLES L. COOPER and his family
moved to Camp Supply, Indian Territory. The first prairie
thunderstorm that swept through certainly impressed his
four-year-old daughter, Birdie. The driving downpour quickly
dissolved parts of the adobe walls and dirt chinking on the
rickety roof of the Coopers' quarters. Birdie's father hurriedly
hung a big canvas tarp over her bed as the "mud rain" began to
flow into the cabin.

This indoor umbrella became Birdie's private playhouse. She
could lie in bed, listen to the muddy water plink and plop onto
the canvas, and let her imagination take her anywhere.

Mrs. Cooper didn't necessarily share Birdie's sense of adventure. One morning she awoke to find that the rain had cut a hole
"so large in the front wall that she could look out onto the front
walk! In desperation she grabbed all her precious newspapers and
stuffed them into the holes between the logs." Lieutenant Colonel
Jack Davidson, commander at Camp Supply, happened to be
walking by and noticed the papers. When he heard her story, he

ABOVE:
Lieutenant
Charles L. Cooper

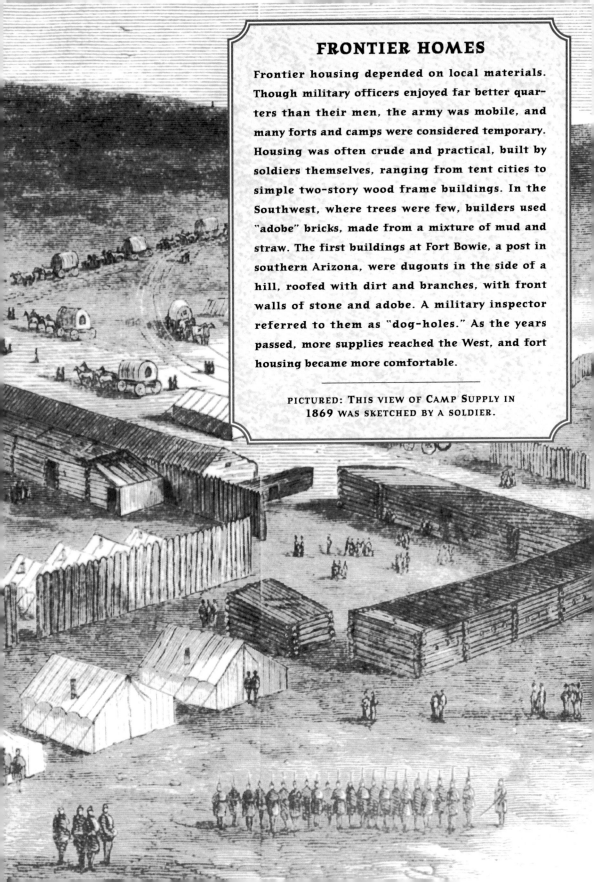

FRONTIER HOMES

Frontier housing depended on local materials. Though military officers enjoyed far better quarters than their men, the army was mobile, and many forts and camps were considered temporary. Housing was often crude and practical, built by soldiers themselves, ranging from tent cities to simple two-story wood frame buildings. In the Southwest, where trees were few, builders used "adobe" bricks, made from a mixture of mud and straw. The first buildings at Fort Bowie, a post in southern Arizona, were dugouts in the side of a hill, roofed with dirt and branches, with front walls of stone and adobe. A military inspector referred to them as "dog-holes." As the years passed, more supplies reached the West, and fort housing became more comfortable.

PICTURED: THIS VIEW OF CAMP SUPPLY IN 1869 WAS SKETCHED BY A SOLDIER.

sent soldiers over to line the walls and ceiling with canvas. This kept most of the rain and mud out.

Mud rain was one thing. A grasshopper storm was something else. The hungry insects would appear in a dense cloud and cover the ground like hailstones. They stripped every green leaf and blade of grass in their path. The unwelcome house guests even invaded Mrs. Cooper's pantry.

GRASSHOPPER STORMS

The 1870s brought plagues of grasshoppers to the Plains. At forts, they destroyed gardens grown to supplement meager army rations and prevent scurvy. The grasshoppers also destroyed entire farms, covering the ground and feasting on crops. Their hordes numbered in the millions, so many that they might form a dam across a creek, or force a train to stop because the tracks were covered with their crushed and slippery bodies. Their impact was as severe as drought, hailstorms, or prairie fires, and the grasshopper plagues forced many farmers out of business.

After one such storm, two older girls about 10 and 12, who were daughters of Lieutenant Colonel Davidson, invited Birdie over to their house to play. The girls had scooped up a bunch of "hoppers" in a big tin can covered with a piece of mosquito netting. They showed Birdie how to tie two captive "hoppers" together with a long thread and toss the insects up to the low ceiling. The grasshoppers grabbed onto a wooden beam and stayed there while the girls placed a third "hopper" onto the thread "swing." Soon the grasshopper circus covered the entire ceiling! They had hours of fun watching the insects' antics.

The Christmas Doll

BIRDIE COOPER NEVER FORGOT the Christmas of 1872 at Fort Concho. That year she saw her first "real" Christmas tree, decorated with ornaments sent from Philadelphia. That was the year Santa brought Birdie a lovely wax doll. It was almost as big as her month-old baby sister. Birdie and her wax doll became inseparable.

If the Christmas of 1872 was special, the following Christmas would prove to be even more wonderful even though her father was in the field on a long patrol. Lieutenant Hans Gasman was in the field too, and his bride was living with the Coopers while the lieutenant was away from the post.

As the holiday season approached, Birdie could hardly contain her excitement. One afternoon in December she came bounding through the front door earlier than usual and was surprised to find Mrs. Gasman in the front room. She was even more startled to see an enormous china doll in Mrs. Gasman's lap.

The lifelike doll wore a lovely white Swiss lace dress trimmed with delicate pink ribbons and ruffles. It was the most beautiful doll Birdie had ever seen.

ABOVE:
Ernestine
"Birdie" Cooper

"Are you dressing that doll for me?" Birdie asked breathlessly.

"No," Mrs. Gasman replied with a straight face. "It's for Bessie Constable. Don't you think it's beautiful?"

Birdie glared at the doll, trying to find something wrong with it.

"Well," she pouted. "*I* don't like dolls with three eyebrows, but maybe Bessie Constable won't mind it." Actually, the doll had special eyes that opened and closed, and Birdie had mistaken the rolling eyelids and eyelashes for extra eyebrows.

"Yes," Mrs. Gasman agreed. "I'm sure Bessie won't mind."

The next time Birdie saw the doll, it was hanging on the big Christmas tree in Colonel Merritt's living room. Because so many of the men were out in the field, Colonel Merritt and his wife held a Christmas party for the families at their home, hoping to cheer everyone up. As the colonel, dressed as Santa Claus, began to hand out the gifts, Birdie glared at Bessie, although the girl had no idea how much Birdie disliked her. Finally, "Santa" took down the big china doll from the tree and read the tag.

"For Birdie Cooper."

Birdie was overjoyed. She looked up at the smiling Mrs. Gasman and down into the blinking eyes of the big china doll.

"Do you like it?" asked Mrs. Gasman.

"Oh, yes," Birdie exclaimed. "It's the most beautiful doll in the whole world."

"But it has three sets of eyebrows," Mrs. Gasman added.

Birdie said seriously, "Dolls ought to have three eyebrows."

FORT CONCHO

This post was one of several that formed a line guarding western Texas settlements from "Indian country," home of the Comanche and Kiowa. It was also a way-station for people traveling west and for cattlemen taking their herds to market. It was constructed beginning in 1867 using local stone, and remained an active post until 1889. Many of the fort's buildings still stand in present-day San Angelo, Texas.

PICTURED: FORT CONCHO'S STONE BUILDINGS

Mouse Fingers

B IRDIE COOPER ALWAYS had a soft spot for animals. When she saw the Fort Concho commissary sergeant about to drown five newborn mice in a bucket of water one day, she pleaded for their lives.

Birdie's father reluctantly allowed her to keep the mice as pets, but Mrs. Cooper said they must stay on the back porch in a box. Both parents assumed the baby mice would not survive without their mother.

Birdie thought otherwise. She nursed the tiny creatures by hand using a twisted piece of soft cotton cloth, which she dipped into a mixture of milk, warm water, and sugar. After a week their soft dark fur began to grow and they opened their eyes.

As cold weather set in, Birdie began to worry that her little pets might freeze to death on the back porch. So one night, after her parents had gone to bed, she got up and brought the box of rodents inside.

Birdie needed to find a warm place to hide her mice, and one of her mother's fleece riding gloves seemed perfect. She slipped

ABOVE:
Mrs. Cooper,
Birdie's mother

one mouse into each finger and carefully placed the glove back into the drawer where she found it. Then she went back to bed. She planned to remove the mice in the morning, before her parents woke up. No one would ever know.

The next morning Birdie awoke to her mother's voice. Mrs. Cooper had gotten up early to go horseback riding. She discovered Birdie's secret when she tried to put on her gloves. "What on earth is the matter with this glove?" she exclaimed.

Birdie yelled, "Oh, you're killing my mice!"

Panic-stricken, Mrs. Cooper could not get the glove off fast enough. In a single, desperate motion, she yanked her hand free, flung the glove down, and fled from the room. Birdie feared her little friends could not have survived the ordeal. Indeed, as she turned the fingers of the glove inside out, five dead little mice dropped into her lap.

Later that morning a solemn Birdie and her father buried the brave little mice in the backyard with full military honors. Mrs. Cooper did not attend the funeral.

BELOW:
Riding was a
common pastime
for army wives
and children.

Single Father

LILLIAN SNYDER was only two years old in 1874 when her mother died. Her father, Captain Simon Snyder, was stationed at Fort Keogh in Montana Territory. After the funeral her grief-stricken father had a difficult decision to make. What should he do about his baby daughter?

Captain Snyder knew his duties as an officer would make it difficult to take care of a child. But what about his responsibilities as a father? He loved his little Lillie very much. Now she was all he had. What would be best for her?

Captain Snyder's mother offered to move out West to keep house for her son and granddaughter, but he refused. Perhaps leaving Lillie back East to live with his mother would be the most sensible thing to do. There Lillie could have a proper upbringing and be well cared for. How could a soldier possibly raise a daughter alone on the frontier?

"We're a family," he decided. They would manage somehow.

Indeed, wives of other officers on the post pitched in to help care for Lillie until Captain Snyder could arrange to hire a full-time housekeeper. Still, when the Captain was called to lead troops into the field, he couldn't help but worry about Lillie. In September 1876 he wrote a letter to his mother about his concerns for four-year-old Lillie's safety. "Lillie was quite well when I last heard but since then there have been several deaths among the children at Keogh. . . ."

The captain had good cause to be alarmed. Each of the Snyders' next door neighbors at Fort Keogh lost a child in a diphtheria epidemic. Luckily, Lillie never caught the dreaded disease.

As the years went by, conditions at the fort improved. More families arrived, and Lillie had plenty of playmates. On her eighth birthday, Lillie invited nineteen friends to her party in the "hop room" at the post. The children danced for two solid hours, Lillie's father noted in his diary.

In their years together on the frontier, Snyder and his daughter had fared well, but Lillie wasn't a little girl anymore. She had become a bright young lady. He wanted her to have a better education than the post school could provide. In 1886, Captain Snyder arranged for Lillie to attend a "finishing school" for girls at the convent Mount de Chantal in West Virginia. The day she boarded that east-bound train, the captain tried to keep his spirits up, for Lillie's sake. He would miss his little girl.

ENTERTAINMENTS

Enlisted men eased the routine of fort life by writing letters home, cleaning their quarters, or gardening to supplement army rations. Playing cards was common, as was singing. Soldiers also participated in athletic competition, such as baseball, horseshoes, or foot races. Posts that were regimental headquarters had bands, and concerts were enjoyed by enlisted men and officers alike. Officers and their families had more leisure time, and their entertainments reflected their higher social status. Wives organized dinner parties, musicals, theatricals, and dances. Outdoor pursuits included picnics, riding, hunting, and even lawn tennis.

ABOVE:
The barracks
ballroom at Fort
Keogh, circa 1890

RIGHT:
A skating party
at Fort Keogh

BELOW:
Fort Keogh, Montana
Territory, circa 1879

Life at the fort changed a great deal once the Northern Pacific Railroad connected the east coast with the west. In 1887, during her summer vacation out west, her father took Lillie and five friends by train to a nearby town, Miles City, Montana Territory, to see a play. When they returned, the Snyders' housekeeper had ice cream and cake waiting.

The celebration was bittersweet. All too soon Lillie would travel back east to begin her second year at the convent school. Her father knew he would miss her terribly. He missed her already. Even though she could spend only summers with him, they would always be a family.

THE RAILROAD

While the train was a common means of transportation in the East by the 1850s, there was still no "iron road" to the west coast. In 1853, Congress authorized the army to survey possible transcontinental routes. Ten years later, rival railroad companies broke ground on either side of the country, with the goal of meeting in the middle. The transcontinental railroad was completed in 1869, but it would be another two decades before railroads covered the West. In the meantime, it was the army's duty to protect isolated settlements and western trails.

BELOW: Main Street in Miles City, circa 1880

Junior Soldier

GUY V. HENRY JR. WAS AN ACTIVE, impatient little fellow. He couldn't even wait to be born. His mother gave birth to him in 1875, two months early. In those days it was rare for premature babies to live, but Guy Jr. thrived. When he was six he survived a bout with malaria, an often fatal disease carried by mosquitoes. Nothing seemed to slow Guy Jr. down.

At Fort Laramie in Wyoming Territory, playing soldier was one of Guy Jr.'s favorite pastimes. He and his younger sister Fannie demanded to be called Corporal Daughtery and Private McShane, after two of the so-called "worst men in the troops." (In reality, the two men were soldiers in Colonel Guy V. Henry Sr.'s command and great friends of the children.)

As far as Guy Jr. was concerned, he was a full-fledged member of his father's command. Guy Jr. even wore a pint-sized uniform complete with corporal's stripes on the sleeves. On payday he lined up with the rest of the men to collect his "pay."

When Guy Jr. tired of playing soldier, he would moonlight as a "stagecoach driver." His stagecoach may have been abandoned

ABOVE:
Guy V. Henry Jr.
about four years old

ABOVE:
Guy's pony "Prince"
was typical of
Indian ponies,
small and quick.

BELOW:
An ice-cutting
party on the
Yellowstone River

in the weeds behind the mechanic's corral. Guy Jr. didn't need a team of horses. All he needed was a little imagination.

At the age of six at Fort Sill in Indian Territory, Guy Jr. traded his imaginary stagecoach for a real stallion, which his father bought for the then-unheard-of sum of $25. Guy Jr. and his trusty steed could out-race almost anyone at the post, where his father was commanding officer.

Winters at Fort Sill were usually mild, but once in a great while a "blue-nosed norther" would roll in and nearby lakes and ponds would freeze. When the ice became thick enough, duty called. The little soldier assigned himself to the ice-cutting detail.

In fact, the entire command stopped everything and made a holiday out of cutting ice for storage. Women packed lunches, and families trooped off to spend the day on the ice. The soldiers used sleds to haul the blocks of ice back to the fort. Guy Jr. probably supervised the men who packed the ice in a mountain of straw, so it would stay frozen well into the summer.

As Guy Jr. grew older, he realized that "playing soldier" was not the same as being a soldier. Soldiering was a full-time job. And punishment for the *real* "worst men in the troops," those who broke the rules, could be grim, indeed.

BACKGROUND: Guy (above, right) at camp with his father (left of Guy)

DESERTION

Desertion was common in the frontier army. One third of the men enlisted in the 1870s and 1880s deserted for a variety of reasons: poor living conditions, low pay, harsh superiors, "gold fever." Deserters might be branded on the hip or put in leg irons—a ring around the ankle with a heavy chain that attached to an iron ball. On an isolated post, punishment for desertion was often at the commander's discretion. The famous General George Custer was once court-martialed for treating deserters harshly—he had ordered a group of deserters shot, then delayed their medical treatment from the company's surgeon.

In 1889, when Guy Jr. was fourteen years old, his father was commanding officer of a troop of African American "Buffalo Soldiers" at Fort McKinney, Wyoming Territory. As usual, he attended the post school, but he had some very unusual teachers there.

One night guards caught two African American soldiers who were trying to run away from the post. There is no record about why the men tried to desert, but regardless of the reason, they had to be punished for neglecting their duty. The guards shackled the ankles of each man with a heavy chain, "as was customary for deserters." This made it difficult for the men to walk and impossible for them to run.

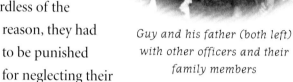

Guy and his father (both left) with other officers and their family members

Since post schools taught enlisted men, as well as children, to read and write, many of the men were literate. Consequently, the commanding officer "sentenced" these men to assist with duty at the post school. These teachers must have made a lasting impression on Guy Jr. and his fellow students, because the men were in the classroom still wearing their chains.

ARMY PUNISHMENT

Neglect of duty, failing to carry out orders, insubordination, drunkenness, desertion—as the crime varied, so did the punishment. The sentence might be extra kitchen duty, a double-time march around the parade grounds, or as severe as court-martial. Sometimes the offender was put in the guard-house or fined. If a noncommissioned officer committed an infraction, he might be reduced to private. Discipline often depended on the personalities of the company's commanding officers, rather than on army regulations.

The Stray Bullet

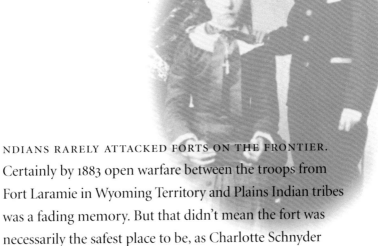

INDIANS RARELY ATTACKED FORTS ON THE FRONTIER. Certainly by 1883 open warfare between the troops from Fort Laramie in Wyoming Territory and Plains Indian tribes was a fading memory. But that didn't mean the fort was necessarily the safest place to be, as Charlotte Schnyder found one day.

Charlotte sat at her desk in the post school, daydreaming as usual. Outside she could hear the daily sounds of gunfire coming from the rifle range behind the enlisted men's barracks. The sound was so routine that the children hardly noticed the shots.

Then it happened. At first Charlotte had no idea what hit her on the side of the head, but it really hurt.

Her little brother Charles, who was in the same one-room school with her, loved to pester his sister. Charlotte thought he might have brought his pea shooter to school again. But the blood running down her cheek told her otherwise.

"Yeow!" she screamed, grabbing her head.

The teacher was not amused. "Miss Schnyder, don't disrupt

ABOVE:
Charlotte and
Charles Schnyder

the class!" he commanded. Then he saw the blood and realized her cries were serious.

"Everyone stand back," he demanded. "What happened?"

"I don't know," Charlotte sobbed.

"Let's see," the teacher said, peeling Charlotte's hand away from her head.

"I know a bullet wound when I see one," he exclaimed.

"Everybody! Get down on the floor. Now!"

"A bullet?" screamed Charlotte.

"Yes," the teacher said calmly. "Looks like it just grazed you, though. Here, use this," he said, handing her his handkerchief.

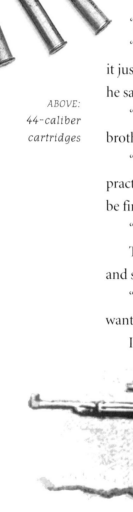

ABOVE:
44-caliber
cartridges

"Indians?" asked Charlotte's brother Charles.

"No," said the teacher. "Target practice. Some new recruit must be firing a bit wide of the mark."

"I'll say," Charlotte winced.

The teacher crawled to the window and shouted to the men on the rifle range.

"Hey! Cease fire, you fools! Do you want to kill us all?"

Instantly the shooting stopped.

"We'd better get you to the doctor right away," the teacher told Charlotte. "Don't worry. I've seen a lot worse. Doc Caldwell will patch you up in a jiffy."

Charles ran to tell his father, Sergeant Leodegar Schnyder, the news. "Somebody shot Charlotte!"

The elder Schnyder didn't wait for Charles to tell him the whole story. He bolted out the door and rushed to the post hospital. Charles could barely keep up with him.

Dr. Caldwell, the post surgeon, was just bandaging Charlotte's head when her father and brother arrived. "She'll be fine. She's a lucky girl. Better take her home now," he told them.

"And Sergeant," he added. "I would therefore respectfully

IMMIGRANTS IN THE ARMY

During the nineteenth century, many people emigrated to the U.S. from European countries to escape war or famine, or simply to seek a better life. A financial panic in 1873 meant few jobs for the immigrants who arrived in eastern U.S. cities. Starting pay for a private was only $13 a month, but regular pay, plus room and board, were reasons enough to join the army. For many of these new recruits, the army provided a means of learning about their new country—how to speak English, for example.

ABOVE: *A soldier's duties included target practice.*

recommend that a different locality be selected for future practices and that the butts be made larger and more secure."

"Sir?" asked the elder Schnyder, a Swiss immigrant.

"He says to move the rifle range far away from the school, Father," Charles translated. "And make the dirt mounds behind the targets larger so the bullets won't ricochet."

"Exactly," Doctor Caldwell said. "Now get some rest, Charlotte. But remember to keep your head up, OK?"

"I don't know," Charlotte said. "Until they move the rifle range, I may want to keep my head down."

POST SCHOOLS

Larger forts with several families had a post school for the children. One of the soldiers usually acted as schoolmaster. Like most frontier schools, the post school consisted of a single room with wooden desks or benches. Texts likely included the following: MCGUFFEY'S ECLECTIC READER, HILLIARD PRIMERS, DAY'S AMERICAN SPELLER, MITCHELL'S PRIMARY GEOGRAPHY, HARVEY'S ELEMENTARY GRAMMAR, DAVIES SCHOOL ARITHMETIC, and the SPENCERIAN SYSTEM OF PENMANSHIP. Sometimes the children of officers and enlisted men were taught separately. On many posts, evening lessons were available for enlisted men who wanted to learn to read and write or to improve their English language skills.

BELOW: CANVAS TENT "CLASSROOM," CAMP PILOT BUTTE, WYOMING TERRITORY

Stunt Rider

F IVE-YEAR-OLD AUBREY LIPPINCOTT was thrilled when his father gave him his first pony. Dr. Henry Lippincott, post surgeon at Fort Union in New Mexico Territory, feared that little Aubrey might get hung up on the stirrups of a saddle. So he taught his son to ride Indian style, with just a blanket and a woven band around the pony's torso to hold the blanket in place.

Aubrey loved to ride his pony, but he was too short to climb onto the animal's back, and he hated to wait for his father or the other soldiers at the post to help him mount. Aubrey was too independent for that. The young rider came up with an ingenious solution to his problem. Aubrey would simply place a lump of sugar or a gingersnap cookie on the ground. When the pony stooped his head to eat the sweet morsel, Aubrey would quickly throw one leg over the animal's neck and hang on.

As the pony lifted his head, Aubrey would fall forward onto his trusty steed's back, grab onto the horse's mane, and turn

ABOVE:
Dr. Henry
Lippincott

himself around. When Aubrey wanted to dismount, he simply reversed the procedure.

Aubrey was even known to ride his pony into the sutler's store to perform this stunt. It may not have been the most elegant

THE SUTLER'S STORE

Sutler was a term used prior to and during the War Between the States (now called the Civil War). After the war, the term became Post Trader. The post trader operated a general store that sold a greater selection of goods than the army supplied: beverages, canned goods, dried fruit, spices, pickles, toiletries, household items, textiles. Sometimes the trader added entertainments such as a saloon, billiard hall, or restaurant. In later years, the army replaced the system with their own post canteen or exchange.

LEFT: ENGRAVING OF A TYPICAL FRONTIER SUTLER'S STORE

way to get on and off a pony, but it worked for Aubrey, and it entertained everyone.

Aubrey and his friend George Douglas, son of the commanding officer at Fort Union, also found an inventive way to motivate some stray burros they rounded up one day. The boys thought it might be fun to have a burro race. They had only one problem: No matter how much the two friends yelled, the docile burros would only walk.

Then Aubrey got an idea. He found some old tin cans and tied a rope to each one. The boys found that if they sat on the

ABOVE: *The post hospital at Fort Union*

ARMY DOCTORS

The medical officer was probably the most educated person on post. The army tested surgeon candidates in their knowledge of languages, arithmetic, algebra, trigonometry, calculus, geography, history, literature, mineralogy, conchology, botany, and physics, in addition to medical skills.

The surgeon was either "Regular Army," or a contract physician, a civilian hired by the army for a specific time period. He might be the only doctor for hundreds of miles, so he treated soldiers, their families, civilians, and Indians.

Regular duties included daily reports on fort welfare, weather conditions, health inspections, and rounds. He was also prepared to go into the field if needed. In their spare time, many army doctors studied Indian languages and customs, as well as local plants and animals, making contributions to museums and other institutions.

burros's backs and dragged the cans toward the burros from behind the animals, the terrifying racket would make the animals scoot.

That night the regimental band was scheduled to give a concert on the parade ground bandstand. Officers' families gathered on the front porches to listen to the music and enjoy the peaceful evening. Aubrey and George decided it was the perfect time to have a real race. The band had hardly begun to play when the burro racers came clattering and careening down officers' row. Aubrey had figured out how to get the burros to run, but he hadn't trained them to stop!

Aubrey and George hung on for dear life as the frightened animals crashed into one another, and then into the chain fence at the far end of the parade ground. It took a while for their astonished, embarrassed parents to untangle the unlucky riders and their mounts. It was not the sort of big finish the boys had in mind.

RIGHT:
Fort Union's
bandstand

BELOW:
Officers and families
outside their quarters
at Fort Union

Telegraph Trouble

L IFE AT FORT UNION was not all fun and games for Aubrey. He also learned some valuable skills growing up. Because of his fascination with the telegraph, he even mastered Morse code.

Before the invention of the telephone, the telegraph was the only way to send and receive information quickly over long distances. Morse code was the "language" used to transmit messages.

The code consisted of a set of short and long taps, with each unique series of taps signaling a different letter of the alphabet. The telegraph key instantly converted the taps to electrical impulses that traveled along a wire. Using a special key, a skilled telegrapher could tap out a message in seconds. An experienced receiver on the other end of the wire could just as quickly translate the taps into words.

ABOVE:
Officers' Row,
Fort Union

Telegraph lines usually were strung along railroad tracks. The nearest telegraph station to Fort Union was at the Santa Fe Railway station in Watrous, nine miles away from the Fort.

Aubrey loved to listen to the staccato rhythm of the telegraph, and he was amazed at how quickly the telegrapher worked.

"Someday," he thought, "I'm going to be a real telegrapher."

The opportunity came sooner than Aubrey expected. One day the army needed to send an urgent message, but the telegraph operator in Watrous had been transferred to another town. The soldiers remembered that Aubrey knew Morse code, so they sent for him.

Aubrey was confident he could send the message, but he worried that he wouldn't be able to understand a reply. Real telegraphers tapped *so fast*, he didn't think he could keep up. Yet the army was counting on him, and he had to try.

With the soldiers from Fort Union standing over his shoulder, young Aubrey carefully tapped out the message. He felt like it took forever, but he didn't want to make a mistake.

Having completed his transmission, Aubrey took a deep breath and prepared to translate the reply. Minutes passed, but the receiving key remained silent. Had Aubrey done something wrong? The soldiers suggested he send the message again. Aubrey did so, a little faster this time. But there was still no answer.

After the third try, Aubrey told the soldiers it was no use. Here was his big chance to prove himself, and he had failed. And in front of the soldiers, no less.

Days later, Aubrey learned the real reason why he did not receive a reply. The railroad had disconnected the wire when they moved the telegrapher but had not bothered to tell anyone. Aubrey had tapped out the message perfectly. It simply never left the Watrous station!

THE "WHISPERING WIRE"

One of the most important inventions of the 1800s was the telegraph. An artist-inventor named Samuel F. B. Morse developed a way to transmit electronic signals with a simple operator key and a sounding key for receiving. Operators wrote or typed coded messages as they came in, allowing rapid communication over great distances. The first transcontinental telegraph line was completed in 1861. During the next decade, the military added a network of telegraph poles and wires between forts and settlements.

ittle Lady

EDITH GRIERSON, daughter of Colonel Benjamin and Mrs. Alice Grierson, was quite a little lady. She definitely took after her mother who knew how to set a proper table.

Alice Grierson's father was a well-to-do Ohio merchant who often loaned money to his children. Consequently she and her husband, a regimental commander, could live more comfortably than many officers on post, employing at least two full-time servants to cook and clean house. As a proper Victorian wife of a high-ranking officer, Mrs. Grierson was determined that her children would have a good education and social skills.

In 1877 Edith Grierson celebrated her twelfth birthday at Fort Concho, Texas, by hosting a grand tea party for ten friends. Her mother wrote that Edith sat at the head of the table and poured from her toy tea set. The responsibilities of the young hostess "kept her busy," Mrs. Grierson noted. That evening the post band serenaded her as a birthday salute.

ABOVE:
Edith Grierson

BELOW:
Fort Concho, Texas

ABOVE:
*Children at Fort
Davis in 1888*

Edith also loved to dance. For her, getting ready for a ball and sewing her gown was half the fun. She and her friend Alice Dunbar, the chaplain's daughter at Fort Concho, practiced hard to master the quadrille, a dance so difficult that few of the officers' wives could do it. Like Cinderella, Edith enjoyed dancing so much that her mother had trouble getting her home from the ball at a reasonable hour.

It was not uncommon for Edith to attend social events at other West Texas posts. In 1877 her friends Mary and Jack Beck invited Edith to attend "Nurseryrhymia," a special play they were presenting at Fort McKavett, Texas, nearly forty miles southeast of Fort Concho.

The genteel invitation noted that the performance would begin at 7 P.M. and that "Carriages may be ordered at Ten." Just where carriages were supposed to take departing guests that hour is unknown. It seems unlikely anyone actually would have traveled beyond the perimeter of the fort unarmed that late at night.

Edith's thirteenth birthday party on August 27, 1878, was to be a gala affair. But for several weeks she had not felt very well, and the day before the party she felt worse. Her parents decided to have a smaller party instead.

Two of her brothers and a few close friends attended. She received a five dollar gold piece from her father and $2.50 and an embroidered handkerchief from her mother. Among other gifts, she received a lovely basket for dried flowers, a light blue sash, a little schooner sailing ship that brother Harry made, and fossils that brother George found.

Edith did her best to be gracious, but she felt feverish and listless. She had little appetite for the melon and birthday cake. Poor Edith could hardly concentrate when the guests played dominoes and a game called "Consequences." By the time the bugler blew taps, it was all Edith could do to say good night to her guests.

During the next few days Edith became more and more ill. The post surgeon finally broke the terrible news to her

RIGHT:
A dance card from Fort Davis features the quadrille.

worried family: Edith had symptoms of typhoid fever, and she was gravely ill. This was a deadly disease she probably contracted from drinking contaminated water.

Alice K. Grierson, Edith's mother

Mrs. Grierson hardly left her daughter's bedside. Day and night, they tried everything to help the girl fight the disease, but on September ninth Edith died.

The Griersons buried Edith in the cemetery at Fort Concho. Soldiers built a low stone wall around her grave. For several years after Edith's death, Mrs. Grierson spent part of each day visiting the little garden within the stone wall, tending the flowers and reading her mail. In 1882, Colonel Grierson and his command moved west to Fort Davis, Texas. Mrs. Grierson finally had to say goodbye to her daughter for good.

BELOW: Fort Concho

ILLNESS AND DISEASE

Post surgeons treated far more illnesses than they did battle wounds. Sanitary conditions at some forts were poor. Sometimes barracks were crowded and poorly ventilated. Few posts had refrigeration, and the enlisted men's food was often poorly cooked. Building sites, logically placed near a water source, might be malarial. (In the 1800s no one knew that water-bred mosquitoes carried malaria.) Contaminated food and water led to cholera, dysentery, diphtheria, and typhoid. Smallpox, scarlet fever, and influenza epidemics raged due to poor sanitation and close living conditions. Childhood illnesses, and even death, were not uncommon.

The End of Victorio

I N THE SUMMER OF 1880, Robert Grierson arrived home from school in Illinois just in time to join his father, Colonel Benjamin Grierson, in a major campaign against Victorio. The Apache leader and his band had left a trail of destruction through southern New Mexico before retreating across the Rio Grande into Mexico.

In July Colonel Grierson got word from a patrol that Victorio and about 150 warriors had crossed back into Texas and were heading north. He determined to stop the raiding once and for all.

First Colonel Grierson set up several field camps to guard the main mountain passes and water holes. The colonel himself led a small detachment of eight men, including his son Robert, to Tinaja de las Palmas, where water only collected after a good rain. He figured that Victorio might just avoid the major water holes if he knew the army was guarding them, and head for the *tinaja* instead.

ABOVE:
Robert Grierson

Shortly after arriving at the *tinaja*, Colonel Grierson spotted a stagecoach heading east along the dusty Overland Trail. He flagged down the coach and asked the driver to tell Captain

Gilmore at Eagle Springs to send the African American "Buffalo Soldiers" of the Tenth Cavalry to Grierson's assistance at once. Later that evening a west-bound stage stopped to report that reinforcements were on the way.

In the meantime, fifteen troopers led by Lieutenant Finley linked up with Colonel Grierson's party. This small force set up defensive positions on a rocky ridge leading to the *tinajas*. On July 30th, before Captain Gilmore's force could arrive, Victorio and his warriors appeared and Colonel Grierson's men opened fire.

"Robert was out in search of adventure and suddenly found it," Colonel Grierson later wrote in his report. The Apaches retreated when Captain Gilmore's cavalry finally arrived later that day, riding in to their rescue with banners waving.

In his diary Robert remembered, " . . . golly, you ought to've seen 'em turn tail and strike for the hills . . . as it was the sons of guns nearly jumped out of their skins getting away."

Colonel Grierson guessed that Victorio's band would try to reach Rattlesnake Springs, another key water hole. Robert and his father, along with several companies of the Tenth Cavalry, raced to intercept the Indians.

ABOVE:
Victorio, leader of the Warm Springs Apache

Leaving the column of supply wagons to bring up the rear, the cavalry covered sixty-five miles of hot, dry desert country in less than twenty-one hours. When they arrived at Rattlesnake Springs, they only had a few hours to set up an ambush.

OPPOSITE:
Buffalo soldiers of the Tenth Cavalry

As Victorio's men approached the springs, two companies of soldiers opened fire. The Indians ran for cover. For several hours it appeared to be a standoff.

Tenth Calvary insignia

BUFFALO SOLDIERS

In 1866 the U.S. Congress voted to create six all-black regiments, among them the Ninth and Tenth Cavalry. The army consolidated four black infantry regiments in 1869 to form the Twenty-fourth and Twenty-fifth Infantry. All these regiments served in the West. Black soldiers often had to deal with tensions left over from the Civil War, and were sometimes harassed by the settlers they were sent to protect. But they were respected by their battle opponents, the Cheyenne Indians, who gave them the name "Buffalo Soldiers" after the most important animal of the Plains.

ABOVE: Tenth Cavalry at Battle of Rattlesnake Springs
INSET: Colonel Benjamin Grierson

Late in the afternoon Colonel Grierson's supply wagons approached the springs. They appeared to be lightly guarded. The Apaches attacked, only to be stopped by gunfire from soldiers hidden in the wagons.

This battle proved to be the last fought against Apaches in Texas. Victorio and the surviving members of his band fled to Mexico, but this time they found no refuge there.

In October Mexican troops finally caught up with the band. Victorio and most of his followers died in that fight. A few warriors who managed to escape would later join forces with the legendary Geronimo for one last stand in Arizona.

Bringing in Geronimo

IN 1885 EVERY YOUNG BOY IN AMERICA had heard about Geronimo, the notorious Apache leader. Or at least it seemed that way to twelve-year-old Charley Roberts.

Geronimo was a Chokonen Apache who was raised in the Chiricahua Mountains of southeastern Arizona Territory. In 1876 the U.S. Army forced his people to give up their mountain homeland and move to San Carlos, a hot, barren, desert reservation along the Gila River, hundreds of miles to the northwest.

Geronimo hated reservation life. So, in 1885, he led more than one hundred of his fellow Apaches off the reservation. The army ordered General George Crook, military leader in charge of the Department of Arizona, to bring them back.

General Crook established his base of operations at Fort Bowie. He also assigned Charley Roberts's father, Captain Cyrus S. Roberts, to be his assistant. The general had been very effective in dealing with the Apache problems. He admired the Native American culture and wanted them all to be treated fairly. They had to understand, however, that they had to follow certain rules.

If he had to fight Apaches, General Crook believed it helped to have some of the Apaches on his side. He recruited scouts from among White Mountain Apache men who had accepted reservation life. The scouts wanted to stop Geronimo because his actions only made life harder for Apaches who remained on the reservations.

The Apache scouts General Crook recruited did not always follow the same rules as regular soldiers. Sometimes they could be just as ruthless as Geronimo and his followers. One day, Charley saw some Apache scouts return to the fort with a fugitive Apache's severed head.

Geronimo and his main band of followers eluded General Crook's men by slipping across the border into Mexico. The general responded by sending cavalry to guard the key water holes along the boundary. That way he could keep Geronimo from returning to the United States.

"General Crook knows the Mexicans are just as anxious to capture Geronimo as he is," Charley's father told him. "Geronimo can't keep running forever."

Sure enough, in late January 1886 a patrol returned to the fort with nine members of Geronimo's band, including the leader's own wife. The group carried a message from Geronimo.

ABOVE:
Scout leader Al Sieber (front center) with Tonto Apache scouts

BELOW:
Apache scouts and soldiers on the trail

The chief proposed to meet General Crook in two months at a place called Cañon de los Embudos, about ten miles south of the Arizona-Mexican border. There Geronimo would discuss terms for surrender.

"It should be a quick trip," Captain Roberts told Charley. "Do you want to come along?"

"Do I?" Charley asked. "You mean it?"

Charley could hardly believe it. Hundreds of soldiers and Apache scouts had been chasing Geronimo's band for almost a year. Now General Crook was going to ride into Mexico with a few aides and interpreters to accept his surrender. It sounded almost too easy.

Charley was so excited he could barely sleep that night. But by mid-day he wished he had. The General's party traveled fifty-five miles that first day, March 23, 1886. Saddle-sore, Charley could barely keep his eyes open through supper.

On March 25 they arrived at Cañon de los Embudos. Charley was allowed to join Captain Roberts and General Crook for the first meeting with Geronimo.

General Crook demanded that Geronimo and his followers surrender without conditions. Geronimo argued that he was completely innocent of any wrongdoing.

The General was firm with Geronimo. "Everything you did on the reservation is known; there is no use for you to try to talk nonsense. I am no child."

THE APACHE WARS

During the last half of the nineteenth century the Apaches fiercely defended their territory—rocky canyons and mountains rough with desert plants—from white settlers. The U.S. government relocated the Apaches to a large central reservation, taking them away from their homelands, mixing together groups that had raided each other in the past, and attempting to change them from mobile hunters to settled farmers. Many rebelled. Among them was a band of Chiricahua Apaches under the leadership of Geronimo, a medicine man. For nearly half a year Geronimo and thirty or so followers were pursued by several thousand soldiers. In 1886, he surrendered and was sent to a military prison and reservations in the east. He never returned home.

BACKGROUND:
Pursuing Geronimo
in the Sierra Madre

ABOVE:
Charley had a front
row seat (far right)
at the parley with
Geronimo (third
from left) in Cañon
de los Embudos. Gen.
Crook is sitting next
to Charley.

Charley suddenly felt self-conscious. He *was* a child, but he surely didn't want Geronimo to think he was a fool. He sat up a little straighter.

For three days the general and Geronimo talked. General Crook promised that Geronimo and his people would spend no more than two years in the East. Then they could return to the reservation in Arizona. However, they couldn't go back to their beloved mountain homeland. Finally Geronimo agreed to give himself up and bring his band to Fort Bowie.

General Crook accepted Geronimo's promise. The next morning the general left for the fort, accompanied by Captain Roberts, Charley, and most of the rest of his staff. He left Lieutenant Marion Maus behind with a few men. The soldiers would follow Crook to the fort with Geronimo and his people as soon as the Indians could break camp.

But when the lieutenant came to the Apache camp he found Geronimo and his men half drunk. The group began their march north toward Fort Bowie, but by nightfall Geronimo had all but forgotten his sober promise to surrender. That night, while the lieutenant was asleep, Geronimo and three dozen others quietly escaped to Mexico's Sierra Madre.

A promise is not always a promise, Charley realized.

Geronimo's failure to honor his word cost General Crook his command. Crook's superiors in Washington insisted that the general demand Geronimo's unconditional surrender rather than honor the terms they had agreed upon at Cañon de los Embudos. The general thought such terms were unreasonable, and was willing to be relieved of his command.

General Nelson Miles, who replaced Crook, had no problem with demanding Geronimo's unconditional surrender; he took a harder line with the Indians. General Miles and his soldiers eventually caught him and his people.

Geronimo paid a much heavier price for going back on his word. The army shipped Geronimo and his band, under armed guard, by train to prisons in Florida. Unfortunately, innocent Chiricahua Apaches from the reservation, including the scouts who had helped encourage Geronimo to surrender in the first place, also went to prison in Florida. None of them would ever be allowed to return to their beloved Arizona homeland.

Was General Crook foolish to have trusted Geronimo? For years afterward, Charley would wonder: What would I have done if I had been in the general's shoes?

GENERAL CROOK

Called "the greatest Indian fighter and manager of the army the United States ever had," Crook saw Indians as humans rather than savages to be wiped out. He tried to deal honorably with the Indians and trusted his Apache scouts, calling them "the perfect, the ideal, scout of the whole world." He did not smoke, drink coffee, or even swear. He preferred riding a mule to horses, and dressed in a white canvas suit when in the field, a "uniform" usually worn by men only to clean the stables.

BACKGROUND:
Fort Bowie,
Arizona, in
the 1880s

Epilogue

AFTER GERONIMO'S SURRENDER, an uneasy peace came at last to the desert Southwest. In the northern plains, however, conflict between the U.S. Army and various Indian tribes continued until about 1890.

As the nineteenth century drew to a close, the U.S. government realized that the army had won the long fight for control of the western lands. They no longer needed to garrison troops there. Company by company, soldiers left the posts, and the frontier forts were abandoned. Some soldiers accepted new assignments back east while others mustered out of the service altogether. Many who left the army chose to remain in the West and build a new life in the territory they had helped to secure.

For more than four decades the forts and their military families helped to bring stability to an unstable land. As these stories demonstrate, the children and their mothers who followed the troops experienced events that young people today cannot even imagine. Some of the stories these children lived were wild and untamed like the land. These experiences enriched their lives as well as the lives of all Americans who have inherited this remarkable legacy.

BACKGROUND: Officers and children in front of their quarters at Fort Laramie, 1889

Thanks to the efforts of the National Park Service, states, local organizations and scores of volunteers, many of the settings for these stories have been protected and, in some cases, partially restored. The following are a few of the forts the National Park Service maintains.

When you visit these forts today, you will stand where these people stood and see what they saw. These sites bring history to life and you to history.

Frontier Forts: Then and Now

FORT BOWIE, ARIZONA

In 1862, as civil war raged in the East, the Confederate government sought to gain control of western territories and California in particular. To protect a valuable water source, Union volunteers built the first Fort Bowie at Apache Pass.

Generals George Crook and Nelson Miles used Fort Bowie as a headquarters during campaigns against Geronimo in 1885, but after the mid-1880s Fort Bowie's role as a frontier army outpost declined. By 1894 the post was abandoned.

Eventually local farmers bought the property, and the adobe walls of the buildings began to decay. In 1972 the site was reacquired by the federal government and formally designated Fort Bowie National Historic Site.

The ruins of the old fort are accessible today by a two-mile trail. Walking along the trail, visitors can imagine the sense of isolation that soldiers who served there must have felt.

FORT DAVIS, TEXAS

Fort Davis, located at the foot of the Davis Mountains of West Texas, protected the road between San Antonio and El Paso. This road became an important link in the Overland Trail to California as treasure seekers and immigrants sought a route that avoided heavy winter snows.

At the height of the Apache Wars, Fort Davis boasted more than fifty buildings and was among the major military installations in the Southwest.

Since the National Park Service purchased the fort property in 1962, many of the buildings have been restored, making Fort Davis one of the best preserved forts in the United States.

On magical moonlit evenings when the fort offers its "Night Tours," groups of visitors can stroll through the barracks and officers' quarters, visiting with volunteers dressed in the period costumes of enlisted men,

BACKGROUND:
Officers' quarters,
Fort Keogh, circa 1890

officers, and their wives. The only light comes from candles, gas lights, and the full moon.

FORT LARAMIE, WYOMING

Fort Laramie began its life in 1834 as Fort William, a civilian trading post. It was one of the few forts in the western territories surrounded by a log stockade. In 1849 the U.S. Army purchased the fur trading post for $4,000. Within a few years military buildings dotted the plain on the banks of the Laramie River, and the fort became a major stop along the Oregon Trail.

Fort Laramie was one of the most important of the western forts. Two famous treaties between the U.S. government and Indian tribes were signed there. The army decommissioned the fort in 1890 and sold the buildings at public auction.

Today Fort Laramie is a National Historic Site. Approximately a dozen structures have been restored and outfitted as they were during the fort's prime. On a typical summer day visitors can watch volunteers dressed as uniformed soldiers going about their daily routines.

FORT LARNED, KANSAS

As early as 1822, caravans of wagons loaded with goods from Missouri traveled across the Great Plains along what became known as the Santa Fe Trail. In 1859 the U.S. Army constructed a temporary post, Camp Alert, to provide protection for travelers. A year later the army built the more permanent post, Fort Larned, five miles away.

Nestled in a crook of the Pawnee River, Fort Larned was also an agency of the Indian Bureau. Each year thousands of Indians pitched their tipis on the plains near the fort to receive clothing, food, and other necessities promised to them under the terms of various treaties.

By 1878 the fort was essentially abandoned. In 1884 private citizens purchased the buildings and land in a public auction and cared for the property until it was reacquired and designated a National Historic Site in 1964.

FORT SCOTT, KANSAS

Fort Scott played a major role in the history of Kansas. During a thirty-year period, the post was occupied and abandoned several times.

In 1842 the U.S. Army established the fort to guard the military road between Fort Leavenworth, Kansas, and Fort Gibson, Oklahoma. Two companies of dragoons, approximately 130 officers and men, occupied the fort. These men were elite soldiers, trained to fight on foot as well as on horseback. Their dress uniforms were flashy and colorful, complete with plumed hats and jackets bedecked with gold braid and red sashes.

Today Fort Scott is a National Historic Site. The town of Fort Scott surrounds the original fort, and the town citizenry is active in the preservation of their community's namesake.

FORT UNION, NEW MEXICO

In 1851 the army established Fort Union to guard caravans along the southern portion of the Santa Fe Trail. The post became the army's central supply station along the trail, providing food and trade supplies for many other forts.

Fort Union was twice as large as most because it boasted a large quartermaster post with huge warehouses to store food and goods. The fort also employed blacksmiths and curriers who repaired wagons and tack for horses, mules, and oxen.

When the railroad was completed and a station established at nearby Watrous in 1879, Fort Union's days were numbered. The post was abandoned in 1891.

Fort Union today is an outdoor museum and a national monument. The National Park Service and an army of volunteers continue to stabilize and preserve what remains as a monument to the men and women who served here.

BACKGROUND: *General Crook (front row, seated with white hat), Charlie Roberts (seated to left), and soldiers at Fort Bowie, Arizona*

Picture Credits

Cover: *Under Hostile Fire* by Frank C. McCarthy © 1979 The Greenwich Workshop, Inc. Courtesy of the Greenwich Workshop, Inc., Shelton, CT; *inset,* Arizona Historical Society, Tucson, 60392. **Title page:** Illustration by Frederic Remington, Denver Public Library, Western History Department. **Contents:** National Park Service, Fort Laramie National Historic Site. **4:** Arizona Historical Society, Tucson, 60392. **5:** National Archives. **6:** *Both,* National Archives; Kintpuash photograph by Louis Heller. **6-7:** *Background,* National Archives. **7:** Library of Congress, Z62-40067; **8:** National Archives. **9:** Photograph by John Anderson, Nebraska State Historical Society. **10-11:** Photograph by John C. H. Grabill, Library of Congress, Z62-19725. **12:** *Both,* National Park Service, Fort Laramie National Historic Site (*top,* photograph by W. H. Jackson). **13:** Photograph by Edward. S. Curtis, Denver Public Library, Western History Department. **14:** Illustration by W. H. Jackson, Utah Historical Society; canteen photograph © 1997 Edward McCain. **14-15:** Illustration by Frederic Remington, Denver Public Library, Western History Department. **16:** Photograph by Edward. S. Curtis, Denver Public Library, Western History Department. **17:** National Park Service, Fort Laramie National Historic Site. **18-19:** Photograph by W. H. Illingworth, South Dakota Historical Society–State Archives. **20:** Photograph by W. H. Illingworth, National Archives; carbine photograph © 1997 Edward McCain. **21:** Fort Concho National Historic Landmark, San Angelo, Texas. **22-23:** Illustration by A. R. Waud, Western History Collections, University of Oklahoma Library. **25:** Fort Concho National Historic Landmark, San Angelo, Texas. **26-27:** *Background,* Fort Concho National Historic Landmark, San Angelo, Texas. **27:** Fort Concho National Historic Landmark, San Angelo, Texas. **28:** National Park Service, Fort Laramie National Historic Site. **29:** Photograph by Williams & McDonald, Little Bighorn Battlefield National Monument. **29-31:** *Background letter,* Little Bighorn Battlefield National Monument. **30-31:** *Bottom,* Little Bighorn Battlefield National Monument. **31:** *Top,* Little Bighorn Battlefield National Monument; *center,* National Archives. **32:** Little Bighorn Battlefield National Monument. **33:** U.S. Army Military History Institute. **34:** *Top,* U.S. Army Military History Institute; *bottom,* Little Bighorn Battlefield National Monument. **34-35:** *Background,* U.S. Army Military History Institute. **36:** U.S. Army Military History Institute. **37:** National Park Service, Fort Laramie National Historic Site. **38:** Cartridges photograph © 1997 Edward McCain. **38-39:** Detail of an illustration by Frederic Remington, Denver Public Library, Western History Department. **40:** West Point Military Academy. **41:** Fort Union National Monument. **42:** Illustration by Theodore R. Davis, Library of Congress, # 612906. **43:** Fort Union National Monument (U.S. Signal Corps photograph, National Archives). **44:** *Top and bottom,* Fort Union National Monument (bottom from Arrot Collection, New Mexico Highlands University, Las Vegas). **45:** Fort Union National Monument, New Mexico Magazine Archival Collection. **47:** *Top,* National Park Service, Fort Davis National Historic Site; *bottom,* Fort Concho National Historic Landmark, San Angelo, Texas. **48-49:** *Photograph and dance card,* National Park Service, Fort Davis National Historic Site. **50:** *Top,* National Park Service, Fort Davis National Historic Site; *bottom,* Fort Concho National Historic Landmark, San Angelo, Texas. **51:** National Park Service, Fort Davis National Historic Site. **52:** *Top,* Arizona Historical Society, Tucson, 19705; insignia photograph © 1997 Edward McCain. **53:** *Charge of the Buffalo Soldiers* by Frank C. McCarthy © 1995 The Greenwich Workshop, Inc. Courtesy of the Greenwich Workshop, Inc., Shelton, CT. **54:** Painting by Nick Eggenhofer, photographed by Joel Salcido, National Park Service, Fort Davis National Historic Site, Texas; *inset,* Kansas State Historical Society, Topeka, Kansas. **55:** Photograph by Frank Randall, Arizona Historical Society, Tucson, 20602. **56:** *Top and bottom,* Arizona Historical Society, Tucson, 19623 and 4284. **57:** *Background,* Library of Congress, Z62-7330. **58:** Photograph by C. S. Fly, Arizona Historical Society, Tucson, 78165. **58-59:** *Background,* Arizona Historical Society, Tucson, 1242. **60:** National Park Service, Fort Laramie National Historic Site. **61:** Little Bighorn Battlefield National Monument. **62-63:** Photograph by C. S. Fly, Arizona Historical Society, Tucson, 78158.